The Five Practices of Exemplary Student Leadership®

James M. Kouzes and Barry Z. Posner, Ph.D.

D1361421

Leadership is a relationship between those who aspire to lead and those who choose to follow. Sometimes the relationship is one-to-one. Sometimes it's one-to-many. Regardless of the number, to emerge, grow, and thrive in these disquieting times, on and off campus, student leaders must master the dynamics of this relationship. They must learn how to mobilize others to *want to* struggle for shared aspirations.

Over the past two decades we've looked deeply into the leader-constituent relationship. Through hundreds of interviews with students, thousands of case analyses, and tens of thousands of survey questionnaires, we've discovered that leaders at all levels follow rather similar paths as they guide others along pioneering journeys. By studying the times when students performed at their personal best as leaders, we were able to identify five practices common to most leadership achievements. We've forged these common patterns into The Five Practices of Exemplary Student Leadership®. These practices are not the private property of the people we studied or of a few select shining stars. They have stood the test of time, and they are available to anyone, in any organization or situation, who accepts the leadership challenge.

Model the Way

The most important personal quality people look for and admire in a leader is personal credibility. Credibility is the foundation of leadership. If people don't believe in the messenger, they won't believe the message. Titles may be granted, but leadership is earned. *Student leaders Model the Way by finding their voice and setting an example.*

> As captain of his volleyball team, Mark Almassy talked about the critical importance of leading by example: "I always showed up early to practice and oftentimes stayed late. There was nothing I wasn't willing to do. I was not

too good to mop the floor or too cool to shout words of encouragement to a freshman. I knew that my actions spoke louder than my words, so I made sure to show people what to do rather than tell them what to do."

Leaders are supposed to stand up for their beliefs, so they'd better have beliefs to stand up for. Leaders must be clear about their guiding principles. They must find their own voices, and then they must clearly and authentically give voice to their values. Yet leaders can't simply impose their values on others and expect commitment. They have to engage others in common aspirations. Modeling the Way begins with the clarification of personal values and involves building and affirming shared values that all can embrace.

Eloquent speeches about common values are not nearly enough. Exemplary leaders know that it's their behavior that earns them respect. The real test is whether they do what they say—whether their words and deeds are consistent. Leaders set an example and build commitment through simple, daily acts that create progress and build momentum.

The personal-best leadership case studies we examined were distinguished by the fact that all of them required relentless effort, steadfastness, competence, and attention to detail. It wasn't the grand gesture that had the most lasting impact. Instead it was the power of spending time with someone, of working side-by-side with colleagues, of telling stories that made values come alive, of being highly visible during times of uncertainty, of handling critical incidents with grace and discipline, and of asking questions to get people to focus on values and priorities.

Inspire a Shared Vision

When students described their personal-best projects, they told of times during which they imagined an exciting, highly attractive future for their organization.

Leaders are driven by their clear image of possibility and what their organization could become. *Student leaders Inspire a Shared Vision by envisioning the future and enlisting others in a common vision.*

> "I soon found myself responsible for leading all these people in a controversial program at our school that had never been attempted," explained Kyle Ozawa. "I needed to inspire my peers with the vision I had. In order for this to work out, every one of the upperclassmen involved in the program needed to share the same vision. . . . I explained why our help was needed and how we had the ability to really make an impact on their lives. I learned that leaders are not the people who set the goals; they are the ones who help people envision them as their own."

Leaders gaze across the horizon of time, imagining the attractive opportunities that are in store when they and their constituents arrive at a distant destination. Leaders passionately believe that they can make a difference. They have a desire to make something better than it is today, change the way things are, and create something that no one else has ever produced. Yet visions seen only by leaders are insufficient to create an organized movement or a significant change in a product, let alone in an organization. A person with no constituents is not a leader, and people will not follow until they accept a vision as their own. Leaders cannot command commitment; they can only inspire it. What may begin as "my" vision emerges as "our" vision.

To enlist people in a vision, leaders must get to know their constituents and learn to speak their language. Other people must believe that leaders understand their needs and have their interests at heart if they are to sign up for journeys into the future. Leaders forge a unity of purpose by showing constituents how the dream is for the common good. Leaders breathe life into visions—through vivid language and an expressive style. Their own enthusiasm and excitement are contagious and spread from the leader to constituents. Their belief in and enthusiasm for the vision are the sparks that ignite the flame of inspiration. Leaders uplift people's spirits with an ennobling perspective about why they should strive to be better than they are today.

 ## Challenge the Process

Leaders venture out. Those who lead others to greatness seek and accept challenge. Every single personal-best leadership case we collected involved some kind of challenge. Not one person said he or she achieved a personal best by keeping things the same. *Student leaders Challenge the Process by searching for opportunities and by experimenting, taking risks, and learning from mistakes.*

Leaders are pioneers—they are willing to step out into the unknown. The work of leaders is change, and the status quo is unacceptable to them. They search for opportunities to innovate, grow, and improve. But leaders need not always be the creators or originators. In fact, it's just as likely that they're not. Sometimes a dramatic external event thrusts an organization into a radically new condition. Therefore, leaders must remain open to receiving ideas from anyone and anywhere. The leader's primary contribution is in recognizing and supporting good ideas and in being willing to challenge the system to get new products, processes, services, and systems adopted.

> "No one was willing to take the time to try and make our idea work," Patricia Hua explained, "because everyone thought that the chances for success were too slim and hence not worth the time. Through my willingness and persistence to challenge the process and do something that had never been thought of or done before, we were able to put on an unforgettable prom. . . . I also needed to make certain that everyone on the committee had this same attitude, and that together, one hurdle at a time, we could make anything happen."

Leaders are early supporters and adopters of innovation. Leaders know well that innovation and challenge involve experimentation, risk, and even failure. Experiments don't always work out as planned. People often make mistakes when they try something new. Instead of trying to fix blame for mistakes, leaders learn from them and encourage others to do the same. Leaders understand that the key that unlocks the door to opportunity is learning, especially in the face of obstacles. As weather shapes mountains, problems shape leaders. Leaders are learners.

Change can be stressful, so leaders must also create a climate in which people are psychologically hardy—in which they feel in charge of change. Part of creating a psychologically hardy team is making sure that the magnitude of change isn't overwhelming. Leaders provide energy and generally approach change through incremental steps and small wins. Little victories, when piled on top of each other, build confidence that even the greatest challenges can be met. In so doing they strengthen commitment to the long-term future. Extraordinary things don't get done in huge leaps forward. They get done one step at a time.

Enable Others to Act

Leaders know they can't do it alone. Leadership is a team effort. *Student leaders Enable Others to Act by fostering collaboration and strengthening others.*

In the cases we analyzed, student leaders proudly explained how teamwork, trust, and empowerment were essential to strengthening everyone's capacity to deliver on promises. Collaboration is the master skill that enables teams, partnerships, and other alliances to function effectively. So leaders engage all those who must make the project work and, in some way, all those who must live with the results. Cooperation can't be restricted to a small group of loyalists. Leaders make it possible for everyone to do extraordinary work.

> "Being a camp counselor for a group of fifteen sixth-graders," Will Cahill explained, "taught me that a good leader is a team player; and to become a team player, one must offer encouragement and be willing to listen to others' ideas. Working with others and getting everyone to participate actively requires trust and expanding capabilities. For example, we gave each kid the chance to lead the group to meals and during nature hikes, and also listen to each boy's ideas. Decisions were made as a group. Another key to success is that in order to gain respect you must also show respect for others."

At the very heart of cooperation is trust. Leaders help create a trusting climate. They understand that mutual respect is what sustains extraordinary efforts. When leadership is understood as a relationship founded on trust and confidence, people take risks; make changes; and keep programs, organizations, and movements alive. Without trust and confidence, people do not take risks. Without risks, there is no change.

Creating a climate in which people are involved and feel important is at the heart of strengthening others. It's essentially the process of turning constituents into leaders themselves—making people capable of acting on their own initiative. Leaders know that people do their best when they feel a sense of personal power and ownership. Commitment-and-support structures have replaced command-and-control structures.

The work of leaders is making people feel strong, capable, informed, and connected. Exemplary leaders use their power in service of others; they enable others to act, not by hoarding the power they have, but by giving it away. When people have more discretion, more authority, and more information, they're much more likely to use their energies to produce extraordinary results that serve everyone's best interests.

Encourage the Heart

The climb to the top is arduous and long; people can become exhausted, frustrated, and disenchanted. They're often tempted to give up. Genuine acts of caring uplift the spirits and draw people forward. *Student leaders Encourage the Heart by recognizing contributions and celebrating values and victories.*

Exemplary leaders set high standards and have high expectations of their organizations. Leaders also expect the best of people and create self-fulfilling prophecies about how ordinary people can produce extraordinary results. By paying attention, offering encouragement, personalizing appreciation, and maintaining a positive outlook, student leaders stimulate, rekindle, and focus people's energies.

> "I felt that many of my coworkers probably felt as underappreciated and poorly respected as I did," Ken Campos told us, but he explained that, as a shift supervisor, he could help to turn around this attitude. "I would constantly extol and commend them for their actions, and more important, I tried to make it clear that we were making a difference as a team. I looked for ways to make our work fun, and whenever anyone did something special, we all stopped to give that person a high-five or a chorus of 'way-to-go' chants."

Part of the leader's job is to show appreciation for people's contributions and to create a climate of celebration. Encouragement can come from dramatic gestures or simple actions. In the cases we collected, there were thousands of examples of individual recognition and group celebration—including marching bands, ringing bells, T-shirts, note cards, and personal thank-you's. Leaders know that, in a winning team, the members need to share in the rewards of their efforts. Public celebrations let everyone know that "We're all in this together."

Yet recognition and celebration aren't simply about fun and games. Neither are they about pretentious ceremonies designed to create some phony sense of camaraderie. Encouragement is a curiously serious business. By celebrating people's accomplishments visibly and in group settings, leaders create and sustain team spirit; by basing celebrations on the accomplishment of key values and milestones, they sustain people's focus. Encouraging the Heart is how leaders visibly and behaviorally link rewards with performance and behavior with cherished values. Leaders know that celebrations and rituals, when done with authenticity and from the heart, build a strong sense of collective identity and community spirit that can carry a group through turbulent and difficult times. Caring is at the heart of leadership.

Learning to Lead

The most deadly myth is that leadership is reserved for only a very few of us. This myth is perpetuated daily whenever anyone asks, "Are leaders born or made?" Leadership is certainly not a gene. And it is most definitely not something mystical and ethereal that cannot be understood by ordinary people. As we said, it is a myth that only a lucky few can ever decipher the leadership code. Our research has shown us that leadership is an observable, learnable set of practices.

In fact, in over two decades of research, we have been fortunate to hear and read the stories of thousands of ordinary people who have led others to get extraordinary things done. There are millions more stories. The belief that leadership cannot be learned is a far more powerful deterrent to its development than is the nature of the leadership process itself. If there is one singular lesson about leadership from all of the cases we have gathered, it is this: *Leadership is everyone's business.*

The self-confidence required to lead comes from learning about ourselves—our skills, values, talents, and shortcomings. Self-confidence develops as we build on strengths and overcome weaknesses. Formal training and education can help. In fact, many leadership skills are successfully learned in the classroom. But training alone is insufficient. We also learn from other people and from experiences. Those who become the best leaders take advantage of the broadest possible range of opportunities. They try, fail, and learn from their mistakes. Leaders develop best when they are enthusiastic participants in change. Ultimately, leadership development is self-development. Musicians have their instruments. Engineers have their computers. Analysts have their spreadsheets. Leaders have themselves. They are their own instruments.

Studies Using the *Student Leadership Practices Inventory (SLPI)*

We translated the actions that make up The Five Practices of Exemplary Student Leadership® into behavioral statements so that students could assess their skills and use this feedback to improve their leadership abilities. The result was the *Student Leadership Practices Inventory (SLPI)*, which has been called "the most reliable leadership development instrument available today."

The *SLPI* lends quantitative evidence to the qualitative data provided by personal-best leadership case studies. If these were the practices of student leaders when they were at their personal bests, then we should expect those people who are engaged in The Five Practices of Exemplary Student Leadership® to be more effective than those who are not. Similarly, we should expect the small groups, work teams, clubs, and organizations characterized by student leaders engaging in The Five Practices to be more motivated and productive. Their commitment and satisfaction levels should be greater when people report being led by student leaders whose behaviors match up with The Five Practices of Exemplary Student Leadership®.

Indeed, these are precisely the findings from our empirical studies, as well as the conclusions from research projects conducted by more than three hundred other scholars and doctoral students (summaries of which can be viewed at www.theleadershipchallenge.com). The Five Practices of Exemplary Student Leadership® make a difference. Consider just a few of the revealing findings documented by these studies:

- *Student LPI* scores of effective fraternity and sorority chapter presidents are significantly higher than those reported for less effective fraternity and sorority chapter presidents.
- Satisfaction by new students with their on-campus orientation experience is significantly correlated with the extent they report their orientation advisors engaged in the five leadership practices as measured by the *Student LPI*.
- The effectiveness ratings given to RAs by directors of residential living are directly correlated with the *Student LPI* scores of the RA.
- The greater frequency in which RAs are engaging in the five leadership practices, the more students living on their floors report being satisfied with their living situations.
- The *Student LPI* scores are higher for those elected student leaders seen by their peers as effective and credible than for those reported less effective and credible.

Findings such as these have been noted across a variety of campus settings and locations, as well as for students from a vast array of both formal and informal organizations. Moreover, the ability to engage in The Five Practices of Exemplary Student Leadership® is not related to following a particular course of study or major, GPA, gender, ethnic background, or personality variable. The desire to lead, and make a difference, is the spark that ignites the flame of leadership within.

Description of the *Student LPI*

The *Student LPI* consists of thirty statements that address the essential behaviors found when students report being at their personal best as leaders. In addition to a "Self" version, the "Observer" version allows for 360-degree feedback from constituents in order to provide a balanced picture of leadership behaviors and constructive discussion of ways to improve.

Responses are marked on a five-point scale, with behavioral anchors. For each statement, respondents indicate the frequency with which the particular behavior is engaged in by the individual. Responses range from 1, indicating "rarely or seldom," to 5, indicating "very frequently." Six statements comprise each of the five leadership practice measures. Scoring software provides feedback along a number of dimensions, including comparisons by respondent category or relationship with the normative database, rankings by frequency, and variances between "Self" and "Observer" scores.

The *Student LPI Student Workbook* provides helpful interpretive feedback and space for students to make plans for improvement in each leadership practice assessed. There are sections on how to "make sense" of the feedback, identifying both personal strengths and areas for further development, as well as advice on how to collect additional information and discuss the data with constituents. The *Student Leadership Planner,* a companion piece to the *Student LPI Student Workbook,* presents a process for continuous leadership development over time and includes numerous specific tips and strategies for learning how to be a more effective leader and to continue to develop and hone one's leadership capabilities.

Psychometric Properties of the *Student LPI*

The *Student Leadership Practices Inventory* has been field-tested and proven reliable in identifying the behaviors that make a difference in student leaders' effectiveness. The *Student LPI*, consisting of only thirty statements, takes about ten minutes to complete. So that 360-degree feedback can be provided, responses from one's advisor (supervisor, manager, or director), coworkers or peers, or direct reports can be generated. With data from over ten thousand respondents, the *Student LPI* has demonstrated sound psychometric properties. (The most current information on the *Student LPI* can be found on our website at www.theleadershipchallenge.com.)

Reliability

Internal reliability (the extent to which items in a scale are associated with one another) is strong. All five leadership practices have internal reliability scores (as measured statistically) that are generally between .70 and .85. Test-retest reliability scores are very robust and routinely in the .90-plus range, with little significant social desirability bias reported. Various demographic factors, such as year in school, major, GPA, gender, and ethnicity, do not play a significant role in explaining leadership behaviors.

Validity

Validity is the answer to the question: "So what difference do scores on the *Student LPI* make?" This question is addressed empirically by looking at how *Student LPI* scores are correlated with other measures, typically of important outcomes such as satisfaction, productivity, team spirit, pride, reputation, and the like. To minimize self-report biases, responses from the *Student LPI-Observer* are used in these analyses, rather than responses from the *Student LPI-Self*.

The evaluations of student leaders by their constituents (chapter officers, teammates, volunteers, advisors, etc.) are consistently and directly correlated with assessments of the extent to which these leaders engage in The Five Practices of Exemplary Student Leadership®. In other words, student leaders are consistently evaluated more favorably (across a number of dimensions) by their constituents as they are seen as engaging more frequently in the five leadership practices. This is a strong normative statement. However, studies also show that leadership can be learned. Any student leader who wants to make a difference, gets good coaching and feedback, and practices can significantly improve his or her ability and comfort level engaging in the five leadership practices and associated leadership behaviors.

The Five Practices and
Ten Commitments of
Exemplary Student Leadership

MODEL the Way

1. FIND YOUR VOICE by clarifying your personal values.

2. SET THE EXAMPLE by aligning actions with shared values.

INSPIRE a Shared Vision

3. ENVISION THE FUTURE by imagining exciting and ennobling possibilities.

4. ENLIST OTHERS in a common vision by appealing to shared aspirations.

CHALLENGE the Process

5. SEARCH FOR OPPORTUNITIES by seeking innovative ways to change, grow, and improve.

6. EXPERIMENT AND TAKE RISKS by constantly generating small wins and learning from mistakes.

ENABLE Others to Act

7. FOSTER COLLABORATION by promoting cooperative goals and building trust.

8. STRENGTHEN OTHERS by sharing power and discretion.

ENCOURAGE the Heart

9. RECOGNIZE CONTRIBUTIONS by showing appreciation for individual excellence.

10. CELEBRATE THE VALUES AND VICTORIES by creating a spirit of community.